THE
POETRY
PACKAGES
Thirty Years

STEPHEN BENNETT

An Awesome City Music Ministries Publication

Unless otherwise noted, all scripture quotations are from the New King James Bible version © Copyright 1982 Thomas Nelson Inc U.S.A. Hebrew and Greek references from Strongs Exhaustive Concordance of the Bible, MacDonald Publishing Company Virginia U.S.A. Dictionary use from the Concise Oxford Dictionary - eighth edition for the 1990's, Clarendon Press Oxford England. Nelson's Illustrated Bible Dictionary.

Original Cover Design - Harry Llufrio, Hong Kong (LinkedIn)
Front Cover Art - Jesikah Faith Bennett (aged 11) *'Girls Just Wanna Have Fun'* Paper collage
Back Cover and Internal Photography - Bernadette Meyers www.breeze.pics
Completed text 2005 - Awesome City Music Publishing
Published by Awesome City Music, 2005 / 2017
Awesome City Music Pty Ltd
PO Box 1312 Dee Why NSW Australia 2099

First edition 2005. Second edition 2017 (print, ebook by BookBaby), audiobook.
© 2005 / 2017 Stephen Bennett, Awesome City Music Pty Ltd

Print ISBN: 978-1-54391-953-0
eBook ISBN: 978-1-54391-954-7

DEDICATION

To every poetic artist dealing with their humanity,
carving out love, walking in the world, living in the family,
believing in the wilderness, wallpapering the caves,
staying in the presence, desiring to change the world.
Continue listening to the river
Create and never give up!

'Still others had trials of mockings and scourgings, yes, and of chains and imprisonment.
They were stoned, they were sawn in two, were tempted, were slain with the sword.
They wandered about in sheepskins and goatskins, being destitute, afflicted, tormented –
Of whom the world was not worthy. They wandered in deserts and mountains, in dens
and caves of the earth. And all these, having obtained a good testimony through faith,
did not receive the promise. God having provided something better for us,
that they should not be made perfect apart from us'

Hebrews 11:36-40.

ACKNOWLEDGEMENTS

The Divine Poet
Our awesome Lord and Savior Jesus Christ
Harry and Mina Llufrio in Hong Kong
For great love, support, and design
Marion Lockyer – Intercession and Prayer
Jamin Bennett – your input and sensitivity to the Lord's voice
Jesikah & Chelsea Bennett – your art and inspiration
Steve Cocking - your input and friendship
All those who inspired me in this 30 year poetic journey

POETIC DIRECTION

"As you gaze upon the cross, and long for conformity to him, be not weary or fearful because you cannot express in words what you seek. Ask him to plant the cross in your heart. Believe in him, the crucified and now living one, to dwell within you, and breathe his own mind there."

Andrew Murray

"Stand at the foot of the cross, and count the purple drops by which you have been cleansed; see the thorn-crown; mark His scourged shoulders, still gushing with encrimsoned rills . . . And if you do not lie prostrate on the ground before that cross, you have never seen it."

Charles Spurgeon

"Jesus taught that "the mouth speaks out of that which fills the heart" (Matt 12:34). We cannot fix our words without first fixing our hearts. When the Lord judges us for our words, it is because He is seeking to purify our hearts. True, the heart is deceitful above all things and it is difficult to know our own iniquity. Yet if we simply pause and listen to how many of our words are without love, we can track them back to the real problem: loveless hearts."

Francis Frangipane Minister

"I do love the image of sheep. You've got to hand it to Jesus. This is a great one, sheep, isn't it? Pigs are intelligent; they are useful farm animals as they wallow in the muck. But sheep! I mean, they're useful for making jumpers, of course they are pretty dumb. The great image of mankind. And they move in packs as well. They all head off in the wrong direction together. There's no particular leader, anyone can become a leader, and anyone can be right for a particular stampede. They're so frightened, and not even aware that they're of great use for making woolly jumpers"

Bono U2

ARTIST ENCOURAGEMENTS

"Treading the path of an artist and as a Christian can be a lonely journey; you live between two worlds, in which neither sometimes really accepts you. It can be like a form of exodus from enslavement, in a world in which art can only be associated with a secular humanistic worldview. Through a desert of often uncertainty and loneliness, eventually the artist does find the promised land...a land that was actually always there, not beyond a gate or a wall, but inside them all along, planted there by God" **Ecclesiastes 3:11a** *'He has made everything beautiful and appropriate in its time. He has also planted eternity [a sense of divine purpose] in the human heart...'* (AMP)

"There are very few guides along the path of this journey. Stephen cries out to a wilderness of lost artists, and encourages them saying, *"It's more than ok! You have it, you are an artist, you are called, destined and pre-ordained for such a work - and even though others don't get you or understand, your work is crucial to God's will on this earth...now go and do the work God has called you for!"*

"Stephen has been one of those very few people cheering me onward on the path of my creative journey, pushing through various film projects. I have felt this encouragement first hand, it's rare, and foreign, and as an artist on this lonely path, it has been like an oasis in a desert."

Angus Benfield - Actor, Producer, Screenwriter, Film Director & Speaker, Hollywood Los Angeles USA. angusbenfield.com

"Prophet, visionary, poet, writer, musician, song writer, teacher; Stephen Bennett is a man with many talents, but deep beneath the external creative work, lies the heart and soul of one who walks closely with Jesus and shares his revelations about life freely. I anticipate fresh insights and words from Stephen, as I know I'll always have something to ponder. I'll be challenged, encouraged, and changed in my walk with God; I choose to be influenced by him. He consistently makes insightful connections between image, life and the Word. He sees God's hand in creation, and reveals truths from nature and scripture which relate to every aspect of life. He lives, breathes, and speaks in a prophetic way, what better than to take his poetic thoughts home in this book 'The Poetry Packages', to savour and read"

Bernadette Meyers - Professional Photographer, Artist. breeze.pics

"Uncertainty and unpredictability overwhelm our world. We have all experienced the need for reassurance in our lives. Poetry is a reassurance. We are meant to listen and read poetry. For inspiration. For enlightenment. For relief. For greatness. For wisdom. For life. Stephen Bennett's poetry will do exactly all of that"

Akiane Kramarik - Fine Artist, Poet, Author, Humanitarian, Philanthropist, Visionary, Futurist, Motivational Speaker, Entrepreneur and Art Ambassador. Akiane.com

"Each and every moment is irreplaceable. We don't need to know our whole life story ahead of time. The blessing is in the peace of not knowing. Yet, being true to the purpose that is given to us, moment by moment. All we have is today, always just today. Today is like a meadow, by allowing today to blossom, and by embracing unpredictable changes that shape our life, we get connected to endless possibilities"

Akiane Kramarik – From the short film of her new painting, 'Today'. Akiane.com

"The Poet Revealed: The Sculptor & The Artist ask us to look and see. The Novelist seeks us to engage and turn the page. The Musician asks us to listen and sing along. The Poet asks for nothing, they reveal themselves through truth; their honest truth, just themselves - alone. No paint, clay, instruments or imaginary characters are necessary. The poet's tools are consonants, vowels, and punctuation; innate building blocks. The poet sets to work, sculpting and painting with language, evoking thoughts, feelings, emotions and ideas; infusing a 'music' within the meter. The melody is our own, we sing to the poem, and the poet sings to us. All born from a symbolic language, lifeless until shaped into the poems form of a unique timbre - carefully, truthfully, and honestly revealed"

"We delve into the heart of the poem to make of it what we will. We venture to see, hear, feel & connect with the heart and mind of the poet; alive and breathing, rising from the page - reaching us, touching us, beckoning intimacy, giving, yet asking nothing. Poet and poem are one within us - truthfully! Within these pages the poet will be revealed"

Steve Cocking - Founder 'SetUp2Worship', Levitical Luthier, Master Guitar Technician, 'Avid Reader and Delver'. @SetUp2Worship

"Beautiful words stir my heart. I will recite a lovely poem about the king, for my tongue is like the pen of a skillful poet"

Korah Sons - Psalm 45:1, a love song. The Bible (NLT)

THIRTY YEARS

PRIME

Thirty years is but a millisecond to God, not even a tea break! In a way, the dates of when and why we create something do become irrelevant, but the real question is; does the creativity endure? This selection of my poetic casting has been steadily and diligently penned over three decades; 1975-2005. I share them with you as if we have walked in them together, as they still echo many things that we can all relate to at any given time.

A few of the poems were written in my late teens, before I came to Christian faith, and reflect early prophetic stirrings, searching, and a valid sense of rawness that still remains current. Most of my rhyme selected for this book, found its expression over those 30 years on this amazing and challenging life journey with God.

In our ever busy, distracting world, we can still take the time to reflect in the rhyme; find hope, and be invigorated in things we all feel, experience, and go through in life. These works are presented in no particular chronology, the dates and years deliberately left off. They are arranged in 7 thematic packages with 23 bundles for you to unwrap anytime.

It is now 2017, the world has changed dramatically since I penned my first piece in my teens, many years ago. Creativity is exploding to new levels all over the world. It is a time to get ready, listen, dedicate, be encouraged and have faith, that the Creator of Rhyme has a plan for your time.

You learn much over the years, and I have found the key to effective creating is to keep having a true worshippers heart after God, so He can breathe art through you. Since 2005, raising children, writing books, and life's many challenges, I still have hope in the future, and that the creative river in all of us will keep flowing. In our lives, we all want to find, and be found. This book starts with a new 2017 poem 'Find Me', that embodies that hope.

May you find encouragement, presence, power, identification, and inspiration, as you discover this poetic gift of 30 years laid open to you in these bundles of my jumbling words.

Stephen Bennett - 2005 / 2017

POETRY PRELUDE

A Prophet – An inspired man or woman that prophesies:
a poet, foreteller or inspired speaker. To speak or sing by
inspiration in prediction or by simple discourse. To show or
make known.
Oracle, seer soothsayer, spokesman, far seeing, revelatory. To
speak or write by divine inspiration.
A person who predicts the future, or advocates a new belief
of theory.
An inspired teacher or proclaimer of the will of God.
Strongs Concordance and the Dictionary

'So they were offended at Him. But Jesus said to them, "A
*prophet is **not without honor except in his own country and***
***in his own house."** And He did not do many mighty works*
*there because of their **unbelief***
Matthew 13:57-58

Poetry is an enigma.

Poetry is a catharsis for the mysteries, the riddles, and the deep complexities of our thoughts and feelings.

Poetry is a beautiful gift from God.

Poetry in its nature is profoundly prophetic.

Poetry is like watching a movie.

Poetry is a warm stream, a tributary: a mode that flows within a spiritual river. It races alongside the various shifting currents of the sounds of music, all things visual, and all things written.

Poetry smiles at paintings, songs, scripts, books, designs, and all things creative as it passes them, live streaming into our spirit from the hidden world - that river is the Spirit of God.

Poets can't stop the river, it just comes, and the pen has to be ready in the writer's hand.

Poets have captured nations, and become icons.

Poets are quoted like presidents.

Poets travel deep, and in their fathoms, hide wisdom, love, and ancient answers.

Poets are colorful, often misunderstood, and undervalued.

Poetry makes more sense after a long time has passed us by.

Poems remind us of our fragility, asking questions, inspiring answers many years hence.

Poems are packages of words and bundles of jumbled thoughts. Let's unwrap them!

Stephen Bennett – 2005 / 2017

Find Me

If I could find you
I would look
Even drain sea and brook
Upturn every stone
If I could hold your hand
Smile and lead you home

I want to find you
But not in fields
Where many heads are tares
Among the shields

I want to wait
To see you shine
From a distance
When I know it's time

Then to me you'll walk
My breath be gone
Then I'll know for sure
You are my song

I've made ready
In the years gone by
Obedience to His commands
Not asking why

I know you'll find me
And we'll be fine
Me and you free
In the perfect time

For He will present
You to me
My heart so full I want to be
Ready for you
I do hope and pray
You find me too on that perfect day

Package 1
HUMANITY

'Put them in fear, O Lord, That the nations may know themselves to be but men' Psalm 9:20

BUNDLE 1

Quest

Force Snatches Thought

More than I more than you
The force pon twitch we rest
We force in zest to procreate survive be blessed
Procrastinate catch colds
Create moulds for things and penicillin
Healing morbid wounds
Women that are swooned on the pile of broken hearts
Feelings that make one move
In the straight line of the rut
The professor they call a nut who knows everything?
Is he closer to the spiritual remorse?

Study eyes and wilted men
Quill a fountain pen to record the life
Oh about the strife!
Things gone wrong gone very wrong
People living in Bill and Ben
Talking to flowers starting mowers
Forces to cut and kill
Milling in the mill flying the horizon
Bloom boxes on the windowsill
Cranberry pie steaming hot

Spirit force invisible like peas in a pod
Until opened like pressed marks on your back
Pushing like balls to its goal
A mouth the whole
To swallow up or reveal the "dark o dark"
T.S. Elliot what a man guffaw
Telling life in an intimate form

Can we tell the scorn we leave?
Will we bereave the bereavement?
Will we live to reveal the course?
Start looking ride that horse

We are Man

Never the End

Groping on a fraying end looking for a lullaby lift
A pendulum swing to safer heights
Knowing the depth of darkness
Serenity of silence
Away from the rift
And the roughness of being alone

Drowning in a worthless sea
In a perpetual incoming tide
Gasping to expose a soul
As rock pools reaching for their share of the sun
Yet grasping on the other hand to hide

Is all a party of fairy floss
Dissolving with a savory touch?
Pinks greens and blue heaven sucked
What is in an empty stick - to point the way?
Bash break or build?
Spin the knife?
Follow intuition or sway with Cabaret?

Tension on a tightrope footloose and fancy free
A fraying heart snaps forever?
Dangling in the big top over red spattered sawdust
Embarrassment to the world but a lesson however

Secure the mooring soul now
Calm the waters in the angry sea
Have faith in the seasons
The enemy seeks to burn a hole in your silken cloth
In the robe a moth in a light free
An appetite so big
City tweeds have been known to fall like flies
Upon an orgy of weeds and gaiety so blind
Who dies?

The blind potter potted
The artist who painted with his feet
The writer who wrote with his teeth
The poor man who gave everything
Art in life
All can all sing - it's never the end!

Jesse's Faith Child

She thought about men, Bill and Ben
Flower pots, the world
When she swirled so young clothed in innocence

She wondered, "If only if?"
"When could be or when now will
To be what was or not?"

She mused on times of fun and prances
The creation of moments
In desires with pieces that start the chances

She pondered on a coming truth
Like a new feather in a flapping heart
Thoughts of lofty things
From where a fragment brought its fruit
From the sellers cart

She felt deep about him the man in her dreams
Drams of Elohim
The might of armored warmth cradling her head
Projections of a future day in the present muddles
In meeting love face to face
Hand in hand reaching back
Smiling forward walking the path of cuddles

She whirred, "Forever more"
Fancies, "Yes forever more!"
Choices obsolete
In straying - the foothold loosens upon the cliff edge
Apple crumble down to a deserted street

She wondered one more time
Her Zoe now in rhyme
Inside of him which somehow was the tree

The bird the hills the sky - Jesse alive
Today tonight tomorrow free
The sorrow passed in wonderment
What will be will be

The Directioner

In the mull of our abode we tangent
Pieces of the cake are waffled down
                    The point evading reach

In clandestine breach
Toxins build inner torments like bullets in the brain
Bowled and hit in continuous takes
Dispersing all reason why one was here in the first place
                              Waste of time

Some turn to religion to digest and not be hungry anymore
There is a point where the bullets exit in every head
A few thoughts taken from the core
Splattered on some off-white flaking wall
The elders in the vast village say so
Happy to pitter and potter
They decay and flake at the eternal lip
                              Dropping dead?

Easy to lay back and let it all happen
We have been planned and categorized after all
However we still get shot at
Ask questions get no answers
To the bouncing ball
The lead gets heavier and the bullets
                    They don't know which way to go

Or do we control without really knowing?
Like the sower and the seeds among the rocks
Yes but those stalks died didn't they?
Like love now and then in the flow
Like stalks it grows in other guises
                              Fertility in the wind

Oh to be a bird to go where instincts go
To know a reason like a season
Always there around the same time
                              Working for Jealous

Maybe that's all
Simple so
But being incredibly intelligent according to the Encarta
We tend to see things in a more evidential way
Ho

I think I've been shot

The Immigrants

Little bald men from mid-English towns
Mid-English frowns in medieval facades
Infatuation abounding upon a three-mile wide
What have you got to hide?

Sausage mash beans and squeak
Dirty men at night who peek

Chimney tops
An indefinite depth of field black in uniform smudges
Forms of lipstick 'Charlie' 'Faberge'
Old gypsy ladies selling violets by the way
Some say, "Coal is running out!"
Little electric carts deliver cream and milk
People dream of silk

Double Decker buses deposit people no fusses
Love thy neighbor
As black and white fray each other's tweeds
In the crush people think of other lands
Of other fortunes
Other little bald men
Who live selected from the sieve
Spending lifetimes in some place
Saying, "Yes!" with grace

So here he was telling us so loud so proud
He did fight in the war you know
I pity the petty refracted from his shining head
Hmm... I was born there too remember
I pang an instant heart of lead

Silent Echoes

What will the next train bring?
What station?
Will he take the stairs that move?
Will it be express?
Shall he stop shall he leap?
Will he stay underground or rest?
Can he run from the ever creep?

Cold smoke breath of a tube
Shadow stands in solitude
Bulbs flicker and crackle
Mass of rolling steel swept in a hurricane wind
In a mind
In the voices that cackle
The clatter of an echoed past

Rhyming Poetry Rhyming

Not easily knowing the next drop of the hat
The wealth of wielding words that swell
On butterfly wings
Drumming vibrations of a mystical past
Knowledge to create present and future tense
Knowing in a poem

Rowing rivers heave ho heave ho!
Hailer blaring minds unthinking
Moving in motion on an ocean of faraway dreams
All going and flowing

Wildest inspiration at the most unlikely of times
Finding a rhyme with the probe of an oar
Reaching high like jumping fish
Underwater eloquence like wishing wells
Peace and quiet no roar

Gelling words in multifarious combinations
Intimate cosmos plotted on paper
A searcher relaxes scratching head
The life of a misty vapor
Merger of senses to sense the common
The common sense?
The Quest of the ancient caper

People

The Worldly Effort to Find Equilibrium with Another Human Being

Tales from trails of needs and wants
Sponged and soaked in an ancient store
From heavy lids and broken heads
Warm bodies and cold beds
The young man in the Sistine chapel
Reaching out to the bearded one
Yet that distance never reached to date
Lost lovers cry, "Come, come!"
And die again
In the equilibrium

The Makeup Artist

Take my hand and leave the coloured faces
Masks of hidden virtues
Walk and shelter
Let the rain of sweet containment
Clean the ravaged city of soot
Painted nails on every foot

Yield to the earthly colors that ache for you
Paint with dancing ochre shadows
That twirl for their own sons
Future gold seams waiting always patient
Smiles of a highlight line way above the crumbs
Like mountain edges through the eyes
In the sunset ends

Your lotus flower
In tones of soft and brushing lids and lips
The secret place
The garden through the cupboard
"Bridge the brow captain take stern the bow!"
Real funny, but hold him in your hand
And pierce the other ear
Leave the colored faces and paint behind your own
Asking questions revealing the hidden midday boxers
In a canvas so very very untouched my dear

Create the hues of ground and grass
Sea and sky blues
Living things and winged thoughts
That fly away so often
Textured grains of swooping fallen sands
Each one recorded as you made them up
Let wild the brush and shush the noise
Stand tall against the tide that threatens
Let them soften
You can
You see

Let go the colored faces
Shine enameled
From darkened dirty unwiped shadows
There is healthy skin
We all pertain to on this pilgrimage
The gloss the sheen the stance
With a gentle stroke and a touch
The world could be your inheritance

Environment

Breathe so Breathless Sweet

Callous sin on Gods earth we dwell
To create a breathless breath
We shelve ourselves
We sit at home sit and brood
Feel our blackened internal jowl
The murmur is but a growl

Mutter and splutter
Mothers breath should bite
Crispness sweet and sharp to touch
Feel a tingling in our feet
Unfazed
Blanket smog descends at night

And we go blind in our haze
Clogging our minds we ache
Cough and curse in rage
The breathless breath

Get out!
Shout and climb the mount
Listen to the timeless whisper
That polishes every flesh and heath
Breathe the sweet
Drink the juice
See the sunshine through the leaf
Breathe

Progress at Natures Cost

We ravish the land from penniless brothers
But are we poor alas?
For he holds timeless keys of others
Machines cannot pry these inherited minds
Some now understand the wickedness of ignorance
In the numbness of the mass

Where are we heading our society why?
Getting worse without notice
Progress?
Our minds are left behind in a cataclysm of wealth
The simplicity and the complexity
Regressing in our stealth

Nature provides all
We are a burr upon her breast
Our natives hold a key for her clean lungs
With a little stir
Perdition of a rash we infest

Piece by piece she dies blackened
Her feelings pinched
She rages opens up and swallows
Freezes heats drowns and blows away
Warning time and time again
Our books on empty pages fray

The wise know
Who fights? Not many but significant as a rotting log
Saving pockets of untouched virginity
Animosity breached in vast lands
We see her love easily found like the love of a lost dog

Real men from mountains and plains have vanished
Not in vain for ignorance becomes understood
What has been done she will forget
It's too late to make amends
We have to stop before we regret - dying unpledged

Man of the Jungle

Orangutan man a man among man
Bulldozers ram
Trees descending falling from an empty sky
Scuttling of feet
Motion in havoc
The piercing cry
Brown sad glistening eyes watch sharp and quick
Eyelids flop in a scratching head
Fleas jump fingers flick

Flowing lithesome in quavers
Through leaves and solid timber
Somehow they remember
Thinking
"Why...running?"
Mind is wrought and wrenched
"Will...die?"
Fleas feast on

Loud crack
Lead bites hard
Dispersing his statuesque mother far and wide
Gone
He falls and cries a whimper forgotten
Sits and waits in history hide
Money is raised to try and save
Fleas crawl on

Clutching hands grope in the hessian darkness
Pig smokes fags
Muffled sounds which
Are sold in pounds to greedy sods
Collar lead and a stuffed up bag bitch

Iron bars and a fad passing
"Why...running?"
Flea suffocates
Drops off

She lay in corpse bits
Her face a hairy lily pond of nothing heaven
"To die - now there's spit in your eye!"

I cry for us and them
You and I
Man among men

Relationships

Past Moves

Moving on leaves empty space inside
Appreciating the having and the beauty
Here but back at where you were
Time settles that feeling you confide

Friends
A memory to see again or not
You can see only you now
You stay a while
You like it
Others logged in a pile of thoughts

Look to the past to look to the future time
What was is often more beautiful and sublime
More magic unlike before
Past perched in conscience exploring the north
Another reality passing by
Home is best and love beckons forth

For some it's their life
A drug flowing in veins
Running
Moving on one step ahead of past moves
You see the past burying as they go
"I was there last year my they were good times!"
You hear it all
One day the move of past will call
Settling
It will make them come just like before

It's calling at my inside wall
Echoing through for more
It's time

Breaking Up

Stunned
By a word and a feeling peeling at skin and soul
Dropped down a black bottomless hole
A non-appetite farce so fast
Behind the past behind the forgetting

Black rubber down inside tight wound
High as a kite
Down fell you
In a Spitfire spiral stopping the surging wind
Viral struck one million-fold again

The witches slicing of the eighteenth century twins
Broken souls floundering in the rough
Summer smooth had vanished
In the glistening tears of a Mexican love song
In the darkness a snail trail on a porous road
Mirrored in the moon
Upset in spears of misted silver seen
Of despair in a pair of tears falling in parallel
Smashing into pieces
Liquid atoms below in the heartbreak
Suicidal soft in its wake
Like hell

When the tide turns to a low with rocks exposed
Who knows?
What could have happened in a hurricane?
In a tidal wash of exposed affection?
Rampaged what a mess

Imagine being deft without feeling
Reeling unaffected in a stagnant line
How sad how bad!
On the other hand with five fingers and a thumb
Bent broken jammed and squashed
It hurts to be the wrong hand

Two points in time are sad glad
Both shed and both cut a ripped shirt and skirt
Mended in time by rhyme
Of some incredible nature big or small

So hanging lead heavy on a chain
With one arm unnaturally stretched to let go
Flushed

The Returning

Tomorrow falls
Chimes complete
The resonance
The unity
Catholic history echoed now
She steps on silver wings
Clutches to the feather down
Bringing forth on the back of the great white eagle

The breathing winds
Her braided hair in exhalation
Striking chords in exhortation
Harmonies in all the men
Of love that she had found again

The beady-eyed bird guided the elemental span
It bore the cargo to the terra firma
She alighted in the light of white silver silk
Splashed with blood
Moving in spirals of grace
Of yearning milk for the male of palmed fronds
Reflected twins in lily ponds
Arrayed so beautified in love
Flamed hearts meeting in violet and gold
Warming worlds now with diamond streets
Limp in cuddles
Graceful holds in skins
They spoke in sparks
Of silent hearts
Forever changed
Murmurs in half closed eyes
Wet

Joining in the rhythm of the dance
Showing
The promise of the return
Whole

The Missing

"Damn!"
He muttered pacing the floor in circles and squares
Spilling tea in plops
The quick cat savored
In raspy slurps off a peeling floor

He dropped into a chair
Installing the cup slowly on the table
The tea leaves were in a position of decision
His mind hummed
Ticking through thoughts
Time passed in heartbeats

He rose
Poured from the pot
Dispersed the leaves in a cascade of slow motion milk

He stirred
Put down the cup
Picked up the keys
Walked out
The slammed door knew where he was going

On the chair the cat slurped
With one eye out the window
Washing the parts

Coming Together

We'll start fresh
Daisies in spring
New flowers
Earth breathing our way in
We'll start together with movements within a universe
In our space
Singing within a centrifugal wheel .
Bullseye no curse
Coils of coils that blend a line of steel

We'll spin like gums in the wind
New shoots and branches fabric
Spinning spokes
The wheel of good fortune
King and queen of our castle
Finally singing our tune
Rulers of the roost
Procreators of destiny
Beyond the Sea of Rhun

We'll cook and sew
Laugh and sing even more
Reap and mow
Tarry parry play with thoughts
Toss and turn considering the unconsidered
Wheel deal
Create and mate

We'll walk forward
A lesson here and there
Bare and skinned but grinning in shining eyes
In the warmth of the cuddle of a bear
We will be
We will be

Didn't Like

Damp carded thuds from ignorance in a hussy body
Green with sickening envy
Enviously green intestinal miles
A clotted gut in a wasted body

Functionally to breed slog
Like hogs wallow in the putrescent mud

Look on the world
Brood and gobble food
With utter distaste

I am sorry you don't pass
This first is a farce
Won't last

Unacceptable
Unimaginable
Unreasonable
Unbelievable

Please leave now!

Package 2
LOVE

'Come, my beloved, Let us go forth to the field; Let us lodge in the villages. Let us get up early to the vineyards; Let us see if the vine has budded. Whether the grape blossoms are open. And the pomegranates are in bloom. There I will give you my love' Song of Solomon 7:11-12

BUNDLE 5

Love

He Dearly Loved Her

Deputy daughter of compassion
The epitome form to men of the time
A crime to let the sun go down
With such warmth dispersed
Affronted in tones of forthright movement
In perennial darkness

Sparkles in the night
People lie in fright
Liveth I

Memories of an erratic past
Like glass refracted in lengthy bolts of passion
Helen of Troy the Caesars of the world
And Apollo in a surge
Could in no way victor this fatigue

Those ravished lands purged by men
Forgotten in the Guy Fawkes spirit
Within the life of the Siamese souls
Joined forever on a cliff upon the blue and green
Within the shade of an Ivy tree
Beside a blue-stone monolith to the pleasant past
Shadows are seen
Slow in frozen motion

Lashes and lids bounce
Sparkles in between
Quivering flesh meets in tangles
The bond is complete as that past could be
Like us to the world
The music of classical antiquity

You

Your eyes
Diamond stars
Mirrored dawning clear morning
Crisp sharp winter memories
Elated breath of the sun upon the sea
Centre of light
Depth
Breathe life on me

Your smile
Moses parted the sea
Sugar snowy powdered white crystalline
Unrelinquished reserve given free
Millions warmed
Millions touched

Your hair
Golden fronds delicate lace
Silky silk in brush strokes
Hues kissed by the sun
Rhapsodies of flight
Head turns hearts undone
A rush in windswept wheat fields
Hot summer days
Tickles in the night

You
A vision
Taken in as one

Your soul
Hidden secrets of harmonized beats
Reaching with natures ever needs of kindness
Love and understanding
I smile and move a little closer

Atoms of Love

I love you darling I always will
My belief in you is still
Calm
Rendering my heart

Forever in my thoughts you will lay
For us are we together
We are forever and a day

We picked dandelions
Love me love me not
Love me

Time is short and our love is bliss
Let go the past
Enjoy this
Deep inside your heart will rise
Life will smile and peace will be in your soul

Our two hearts make a whole one
I love to love the love I love
For all eternity under the Son

When we keep coming together
Love will always manifest

Finally when the door comes down
You will go through and join me
Take my hand
We will walk the long and windy road

The Golden Ring

The Golden ring was anchored
Finger jetty held the ropen coils
Timeless foils
Of interchange
Of wealth and stealth
The unnerving spark of Godness
Passionate in health

A gift of love
Unexpressed in seeing tone
Tear drops in unison
Held together from the earth
In the colors of the perfect sun

Telling of binding
An unbending force seeking itself
Warmth and heart felt creams
Flowing in pastels through thousands of miles
Thousands of dreams

A meeting
Yearning and committing
Remitting all the unworthiness
The fight through time
Claiming a charge on inner secrets
Tuning it all to fine
Telling of the prophet and the prophecy
That its textures will reign supreme
From the artist that is divine
For the artist that is clean

It is?
It will
It completes
Trimming circles
Ballet cycles
Lemniscate coiling of the golden ropen anchor

The Lady

What's more a finely fortuned silkened sigh
A memory by and by
Fillyesque aplomb at food
A Tower of Able perfect at table
And talking in the mood

Wooing wooish wit from the whimsical man
Her heart beat the 'Can Can'
Tapping on a polished floor
Leaving a multi shoe print on an ever open heart
Legs through an ever open ever willing door

Gold could only do for the queens of old
Like that to behold
An embrace of silent wetness in aching smiling hearts
Again another race to bring some peace to the world
Harkening unto its darkened paradise
Where decrees are opened and carefully unfurled

She feels that gentle yearning
Ripple her tender shores
Let him dive and splash
Stroking the open pores

Under over in and round
The dolphin man in playful sea
Who knows the secret of what all of this will be?

Creating thoughts she danced
Balletesque Romanesque
A puff of dreams
Spiraling on a pink satin toe
Spinning spinning she vanished to a world beyond
And all those thoughts below
Where smiles were smiles and handed hands glowed
Where lips swelled and long boats rowed

"No matter" she thought

Mesmerized

I have known the faces of many
I have felt the surge and sigh
Of a moving ocean and a gull
The winds that cleansed and combed me dry
Crashing the storm on the sailor's hull

I have stood high upon a mountain
Blown bubbles at the fish beneath the sea
Felt love

The sun is shimmering
Upon the early morning chirping
Between a swelling mountain
Majestic trees waving

In giggles
Diamonds danced upon the dew
My shoulders bronzed

The woolly nimbus formed your face
And you slowly drifted by
Rich melodies of thought
Your warm breath upon my brow had left its mark
I heard heaven sigh

I gazed upon my memories
I had felt them move
It purrs to be content

Stand by Me

The equestrian flight
On a mounted messenger which stood the test
Of a fallen winged night that rushed
Flood pon flood on a world noir
The scar in hand that carved the keys from Hades

High He rode gathering elected to the light
As moths in heated night did come in air to meet
Shining wings of armor dancing in the colors
Je t'aime d'amour in a world noir

Stood He stands on Zion's crack
Never in the split to be
She stood with me

My filly my friend
Firm in arms that knows
Equestrian mount of mine
Committed to the jump of timeless time

We stood against the world noir
We tied our yellow bows
No scar to big
It's the equestrian flight we chose
Stand by me

Love Just

Love just walked through sliding doors
Embracing sun
Caressing on tiptoes of tenderness
Deep inside the city heat of London

Her Spanish thighs and pores
A myriad of pools in skin
In the underground that chattered
Beneath the waving of her dress
We were all transfixed with smiles
In remembrance of where we all had been

How refreshing to behold such d'amour on a train
Way below the earth in tube
Underneath above
Where so many scratch around in vain

Purest affection at peace in the smitten
The Danite hand so tender
Around the girth of thousands
Of the wishful brides of Britain

Through sliding doors they blew
Transparent in transport glass
In slowing motion they danced
The glances
The white teeth
The eyelids
Oh nothing!
Nothing whatsoever to hide!

The Fragrances linger
Yes even now
An expressionless Indian stared vacant as a Lot
Where agape had been to sound
In a flash his finger jabbed in open
His heart of aching sores
From idolatry and poverty
In a flash he was gone behind a million sliding doors

The posters shimmered in the product sheen
As another man passed them by
Where those had slept in an old war gone
We travel and we die

I saw God in them
In two who loved
No meetings rules controls or guns
I saw just a touch or two
A kiss a smile
God's intimate love on the run

The pain of Kosovo bombs and the debt
Was now a distant dream
As lighthouse fingers moved
On a wet tropic sandy shore
In an instant the tube seemed
Transfixed and held inside that roar

Nothing added
Nothing taken away
Nothing on file
There were no chores
Just was
And the magic enthralled the tunnel sons
When love just walked through sliding doors

BUNDLE 6
Passion

Eye of the Night

Night one

In the full moon in the arousal of the night
In the full moon she stood grasping
In the full moon it had been a long time
In the full moon he had no choice
In the full moon covered
In wet crystals of golden beach
In the full moon within the aching scream
In the full moon romantic tenderness
In the full moon adolescents
In the full moon they fell in slumber
On a polished floor

Night 2

The sad figure sits with ponderous gazes
On an empty sea
Unmoving except the wind dancing with his hair
Frilled edges of a breathing ocean brushes the earth
Filling the gaps in the cracked heart of a storm
Ravaged land
Inner nightmare

Shell gifts
Pearled presents in the handmade uniqueness of time
Glistening on a golden band
In eight point stars in the wax of a full moon
Pieces of a sad soul
Run in salty droplets down a sad face
Ringed and lined through a sad mind
From sad eyes
Like gift card cats
The Eye of the night watches knowingly
Wearing one of many hats

Yearning to Know

Growing pains and whispers
The anguish of lost embraces
In a time when fireworks were a specialty of the house
Like the mouse that lost its hole
Bunged and mussed to find another home

Sweet embraces
Reflected in the warmth of a charcoal flame
A jeweled tear twinkling in the eye of discontentment
Characters were born of love like the thirties dreams

Reams and reams of philosophic themes
Untied and tied each time
A new thread of learning
Yearning to know the secret of the jewel
The secret of the everlasting rhyme

The New Night

Regency rooming romance
On a crooning winters night
Late with quiche and muddled thoughts

"What thou ought do
When winds of soul are warm
And the breeze of minds are wrought?"

Parked in thought six stories high
The closer to the sky the better
To fetter fluttering hearts
On the wings of a winter wind

Classical violins caressing peeling skins
Groping for garden songs that blends and bends
In heated soft and wet caress

Fireworks and bombs
Every breath full and fast

At last

Sleep in deep
Morning sun arose to newly wake

Intimacy

In Memory 1

In memory of you
Meandering walks in magical nights
Making bread
Words that were said
Feelings
The notion
Making love in slow motion
Whispers sighs
Touches cups of tea
Smiles we did give
Eyes we did see
House we live
We shared all those things

In Memory 2

He hit his head and squeezed the bag into the cup
How she disliked that
The squeezing that is
It was tea to be milky flat

Poor dear hurt his fingers
She sighed
Stroked and squeezed them
She cared

Alone he cried

In Memory 3

Wanting to see you smile
Talk and grin
Laugh walk
Begin to dream

To see you breathe
Smell and touch
Listen
Feel much of me
To see you drink
Eat and cook
Ask
"Quick come and look!"

Seeing you care share and love
Write with the flair of an ancient scribe

To see you clean sheen standing tall
Adhere things high upon the wall
To see you match and create
Want
Shout and grate cheese
Apples carrots and all those lovelies

To see you close open show
Come
Water flow and sunshine

To see you standing still
Looking
Bare
For me to behold

To see you
Wanting

The Dinner

For what we are about to...
In floppy slothful motion lidded movements
He raised his head
Eyes shone as lit crystalline
Before him the purest woman of many a dream
Statuesque erect feline elegance

The flame of candle lit the flickering night
Waxing cream softly dripped
Nourishing art framed in cotton wool haze
Of warm tongues licking knives and forks
Peace and aching as the butterflies flew with pollen
Through the seeking maze

She playfully wondered inevitability
Her tawny bronzed hair
Flicked by an exacting wind from nowhere
Deeply set in brun she twinkled in the subdued glow

A flash flooded with fine wetted gazes
Warm watered warms
In a heated seat

Passion waxed
Desert flowed

Arousing full moons laying dormant
For the moment of unfolding
In a blissful line
Of blissful blisses

Not Alone

Love lay bare
Feeling the scorch of the eternal fire
Apart but not alone
In the land of Eire
The winged dove took flight across the sea
The female knew this was meant to be
As the pruning of her wings
My she was a sight

La petite sigh la petite groan
In the memory banks of the cosmos answer
A new upturned stone
It was not by chance love had flown

The minutes of the meeting treasured
The nest a bed in wanting
A mating call
The inevitable homing of lofty migration
The gathering of all

Into the sunset here
Into the sunset there
Really just the same

Beyond that a spark
Someday moving us all

BUNDLE 8

Friendship

The Eyes of Friendship

A full tight canvas
The friendship sailed
She pounded his sturdy rig
Strength of a chain-mailed age
Like a Lebanon mast
Like the wisdom of sage

Outstretched arms
The trade winds of tomorrow
Billowed full they draw the cords into knitted folds
Like the willow needs the wind to brush its fronds
And feed the hollow

Waters of the sea of ages wetting
Washing salt
Earth creaking timbers
Strengthened by the wisdom of the wind
In mirth of fathoms free
Way below
Touched only by that lamp at night
Of inner winter glow

The eyes of friendship twinkle in the midnight
Orange hues of Captain's cabin windows
Naked shadows in lead-light icons
Knowing as he carries the bow of life
Plunging rising
A dove ascends and nestles in the nest of crows

No friendship sails without her
But stands anchored in the bonds of chains alone
Dead sails
Rotting timber joints
Time eats a never-ending appetite of broken stone

The friendship sailed its perfect work
Slipping through oceans of highest majesty
By and by she snuggled warm
In the Root of the Ageless Tree

A canvased arm soaked in oil
Protection from the spice-less ice
Together billowed at full tip
With all the ropes of coil

Living in the eyes of friendship
The wedding and the rice
There's no other way to be
Nothing will suffice

Package 3
YOUNG

Young Love

Besotted Love Letter to the Princess of Kew

To my dear picture of wonderment
What tis pon thine eyes?
Pon twitch I have cupped mine lips
In love and tears from thee mine one
The thunderous river from whence they flowed

Do thee sparkle today much like a mirror?
Reflecting thy raw red passion
Of that seething volcano within thy heart!
Undoubtedly mine love of many times and cherishing
They do

For thee mine eyes wash in blue
The color of Neptune's land
I hold mine hand just to glimpse
To catch the threshold of thine heart
I apart will forever be within thy soul

I have such memories of the time we spent together
Making music with our love
Pulsating harmonies
Heat of fire burned hearts from a flicker
Pon whence we set our eyes pon one another

The times we caressed and messed our hands and…
Oh yes I remember dearly helping thy mother
Make apple pie
In that kitchen how we laughed!
Together we sat upon the secret lawn licking dry
The tools that built mankind

Ecstatic my love was the feeling
Whenpon thy sent the pelt of parchment to mine door
Withholding a painting of thyself
Yesterday ago pon May and
Just for me!

Did make me refract thought pon thought
The surge within my heart
Came flooding back in tidal torrents
As I hung
As thine should
Picture pon mine wall between the posters

The roses in the garden are beautiful
For it is spring now and everything hath blossomed
Like pon thy love
The countless shapes of petals carpet the ground
I hope thee dear sing the colors of their beauty and...
What the oracle said was true
That we shall meet again mine dear
When all this strife of war is through

I hope thy find mine message sweet
As I send this parchment
With lavender from the garden
Send thy message soon mine love and...

In love your fondest in your bondage I lay

Young Love in Six Parts

part 1
Two of us could share a love like nothing else
But I have to leave to search
I stretch and bond with every passing mile
Missing missing
Your smile ponders me

I do not know you well but well enough to know
Hidden in your heart is a secret like a legend lost
Soon we will meet again sharing what we had
Do you hope like me?

part 2
At night I think of you like days
Hazy mind a whirl of things
I'm lost like in a maze of rings

Shall I go back to her or follow the land?
I mope
Think and feel
Feel and think
Scrape the air
Go boy to the horse's mouth!
Go back go back
The adventure won't go away!

part 3
Love will be somewhere
I do not know I cannot see
Sometimes I find
It stays for a while
Then often empty ground
Why does this love die?
To put it aside on a remembrance pile
Where's the real that seals forever?

I find the one
Feel and stray
Confused and young
The older know?
Time will knit the fray they say
Young and foolish
Hey that hurts!
Take it in my stride in learning
Experience guide me
Make wise my yearning

I have found it now you know
At least I think so
Anyway she is fine and I feel...
Oh dear here we go again

part 4
Faraway earning big money
Heavy heart
I left my love for this...
She reigns so clear and constant in my mind
There is no other
I must go back
What about the money?

And I'm in love?
Paper takes the weight?
I'll take this golden-gate and...
Chuck it for all I'm worth!

What the hell am I doing here?
Splashing paint and beer
I should go back
Ten minutes over...back to the grind

part 5

Are you in love with her or in love with love?
Did I love the feeling?
Miles away by the sea the question
Like a ceiling it was empty without her
Clearly in my mind a secured soul
Like a foal on jellied legs

part 6

I came back to her for what?
Dwelling on it all that time
The talk the highs and lows
Silly sot it's over
In two days I see a child
A pullover
A fool in romantic pursuit

Feelings a miss-guide
Illogical logical decision
I wasn't sensible
Hard way learns again
Put my heart back in prison

"You will find out!"
"Yes I know," I shouted
Waving from the plane
You do with a grin on your face
One's own heel marks embedded behind
Smacking at the pain

A friend away left
Me well back at the start
Here I go again
Wiser in time I hope
Let's feel again
Whatever
To yearn young

BUNDLE 10
Student

Studying the Biological Mess

Pencil cases
Thick books rulers and lead
Soggy biscuits swimming in the saucer of tea
Black bags on a studious face
Sigh's huff's and puff's
Writing flows in colored pens
Solving cellular problems on cartridge
Glancing up at me

Doodles by the diddlings near the scribblings
Feet that twiddle under legs of chair
Sticky fingers thinking through hair
Sniffle snort the books rapport
Crumpled yellow tissues

What's in this fissures fact?
Loose leafed crumpled straight and narrow
Outside the sparrow twitters
Her mind a carousel of cells and shapes
Numbers formulas swims and webs
Study jitters

Leaning elbow
Hand on temple
Hours on end
The bend the straight
She leaves to fate
To pass the test
To check the mess of logic

BUNDLE 11

Growing

Twenty One

Cycles of livelihood breath unearned
Evolutions of the experience
Twenty one
Not yet burned

The third round of mystery seven
Adult X
Man six six
Woman a woman
Soul a soul
Revolution coup d' youth
Horse from a fallen foal

Time
A measure that flies slips and ticks
Leaves none at all
To lose the atom the moment the birthday
An age an eon an ilk
Completion on a successful road
Nine to grow older
Still and smooth as silk

Twenty-one is a moment to stand tall
Like candles on cream
Or cower in mans whimsical desires
Or die in the deceiving dream

Forthcoming years
Now open the door with the city key
If you dare
The wheel is thrust in the race of human failure
Your will...or
Truth as He sees fit?

Package 4
WORLD

'Do not love the world or the things in the world. If anyone loves the world, the love of the Father is not in him. For all that is in the world - the lust of the flesh, the lust of the eyes, and the pride of life — is not of the Father but is of the world. And the world is passing away, and the lust of it; but he who does the will of God abides forever' 1 John 2:15-17

Temptation

Temptation

Subtlety of silence creeping to test
Bad or best
Right or wrong
Good

On a golden thread sowed
Bad piled high on a plate of gluttony
In blindness to the unmined reef
That glowed

Listen in
Fear not the faith but for the hiss in the dark
"The dark o' dark"
Venom penetration dimming lamps
Make's you eat and lick the plate
Will churn and belch knowledge
From your knowing lip
Leaving a flicker of filament as a delicate nervous
The price set at the highest rate

Listen listen listen
Do not let the glisten of secretion whet your appetite
Get thee behind me Satan
Keep feet in soul where no angels fear of treading

The offers are sweet sack roses
Soft as hay in spring
A golden plaque of dissolving promises
Decay only rotting

The blind white stick sucked thin like Brighton Rock
Callused hand revolving
Feet firmly stuck in stock

In the hiss
In the dark

Listen listen listen
Cast enchantment aside
You can walk
Your two feet can meet Him
To make ends meet
Don't hide

Listen
The hurdles never end around the bend
The potholes to rip and wrench
It's the Jack in the sand or be firm in the Rock?
Decisions
Many decisions around the clock

Listen
The Invisible Man voicing in ribs
Watch the hiss of femme fatale
Grab the Golden Thread
Swing like Tarzan
Tick like a pendulum
Feel the kiss of a long long long breath
Lead us not into temptation

BUNDLE 13
Religion

Headlines About Nothing

A breach of faith?
Oh dear!
The Catholic priest fell in love and wanted to marry!

World shaken now doors locked
Collar tagged dirty filth
Topless beaches defrocked
Bottomless cups of coffee at The Universal McDonalds
Hot
The black britches don't fit anymore
Life rocked

A penis unlocked from a demons impish grip
A fountain free to explore Shulamite's garden
As it should be
If he had only read the fine print in Tim's Greek
'Bishop blameless...husband of one wife'
Padre Luther found out and had six children
Started a revolution
Changed millions for Life
The liberty solution

Illusory trust in bricks purple and scarlet
Cynical love
That word is four letters of frustration
The golden keys and beads to golden things
Essence of religion leading to black dresses
Sodom and aching foreskins
As many have testified

"Let it go let it go let it go!"
Enter the struggle over seventy two months
But he fathered a child in yesteryears
To another fatale femme!
"Oooh! Can't forgive that can we me precious!"

The desire so godly
So misdirected
So misrepresented
What does one do with stiff gift?
He needn't have suffered at all really
He could have bought instead he rented

A busted needle now pierced
A muddied institution full of mud
Predictable conclusions to the illusions of centuries
The silliness of Elmer Fudd

A breach of faith?
Papal bull!
Sincerity inside a nutshell
Blinking eye lids and false plastic smiles

Woven fingers and a confessional box
He needs the yellow pages or a directory of some sort
Words will kill the lies of the red-horned fox

It's really a joke
The father can be proud and humbled
The husband of one real wife
Call no man father
Call every man a lover
The Lover has spoke
God the real Father
Really... doesn't mind
At all

Broken Sundays

Broken Sundays families yearning
Happy Mondays around we go
Again traversing the flying Maypole
Will it stop the broken-arrow?

Weeks go by where are the people?
The park is empty my heart is full
Magazine is glossy glossy
Beckoning our senses pull

Control the temperature regulate the grind
Looks all too familiar now
Snapped in fragments Sunday Sunday
But I do not mind or care somehow

It's time to peel corrupt veneer
The worship of the sun
Oh that sacred day
That means not much
On a broken Sunday morning crutch

The devil loves the worship
He loves all the spirit pomp
Like an ass that speaks English
The smell of a broken service romp

"Oh didn't we have fun!"
Woe unto us - are we blind?
Humility and the heart of the Father
Now - what else is there to find?

His will no doubt to mend the cracks
The wall that saddens me with woe
I've supped this cup long enough now
It's time to go broken Sunday
It's time to go

The Eye of Suspicion

I saw it at the party
Eye in a pasty ashen face
Famous yet friendly
Only for a moment
Until a well rehearsed distraction
It was a lonely soul
That only knows the lies and rumors
If only the eye saw me in the heat of my hot coal

It looks through mist
Cataracts alive swirling in demons
It chats around the edge
It smiles from behind a curtain
Loves with condition
It's the eye of suspicion

If you knew me in my desert
Then we could truly be friends in the call
What we know and understand
Could be shared with all
But alas
Transparency is something in a camera
Love is something in a book
Suspicion is a lie
You can see it in the look

The eye is dark yet blue
The eye does not believe in you
The eye knows words from many others
But never asks the horses brothers

What manner is behind the pupil black?
A hole of fathoms deep
Singing to the world from blue
I wish you could see the truth inside
The things that I keep

From a distance they look at your mountain
They do not know the fire you stroked
They've never climbed your rocks
They've never seen your view
They've never felt the breeze
Of the planted flag for you

The eye stays locked upon the fence
Rodeo that was never rode
Bull that was never bucked
They've never tasted real war
They only know your supposed offence
Only know where you've been tucked

Ones that you wonder, "What?"
In the eye of suspicion
Veiled in cool neo nonsense
On top of the attrition!?

When you stand tall - many point
Sharp are the nails of liars
In the coffin of your desires
The Gravedigger digs
You walk down in the soil
On stairs so moist as dust fills your eyes
The figs have all died
Covered in red
All is black
Still and dead

In time the green blade
Wields its timely cut
You emerge in a new field
There are new animals
In a new fence
The eye you saw has gone
A bird sings cadence
And you know
The Eye of heaven smiles along

BUNDLE 14

Virtue

Know in Silence

To feel the need of silence
In the kingdom of my space
Unencroached privacy
Home the sweetest place

Of love
Of peace

To be unblemished from leeches
Cascades of crowded spaces
Intruders
Marauding faces
Pinching numbing
Reining in your bit
Blood on your teeth
In the breaches
And the britches
That don't fit

To know
The outburst of a fully standing man
To relish here
In a quiet sphere In
His silence

Of love
Of peace

Three Sides of the Healer

Sleek ancient oil
Soothing incessantly the ills of old
Delicate as glass
Blown and sculpted color
Bold as brass from a well of potted gold
A League of Nations
Waiting for the fingertips of the returned
The spy coming in from the cold

Raunchy rough riled
Conceiving forsaken
Making efforts at climbing the ladder of Jacob
Sumlong some short like dry rice in the wind
A rapport of zealous locomotion
Like an ocean's many faces and the stars
Challenging the challenge
The principles of Mars

Strong meek persistence to search
Moved within and without
Emotions swimming
Get out get out

Blade thrust
Withdrawn again
New leased life on shore
Water and blood from a locked in hymn
An unwanted thorn
Androcles removed
Life learnt to love the Lion
Thankyou George Bernard Shaw

BUNDLE 15

World

Sight at Night

Hitching a ride along a city street
Cold and ruffled they pass
Phobias to violence incomplete
Secure behind metallic doors?
The wheels of time don't stop this mechanical farce

Woolen teeth bite against the invisible ensnarling blue
Seen in the piercing lights
Caressing you
Coughing up nature's imbalance
Watering my eyes
Pricking throat
Paining brain
The odds increase with the blotting of darkness
Thunder cracks
Down comes the rain

Woolen coat wraps
A horn blares
Someone nearly smashed a door
Rubber burns water sprays
Heads turn in pub
From inside Toby's amber fluid jug
Mesmerized intoxicated more
Peering through the lead light window warmth
Trees with ferns whip wild in the watery night
Homeward beings bound in flight

Legs walk
In Toby's people talk in humming sounds
Lipstick stick and nicotine grounds
Blank stares
I don't go in
I follow the rain in this pain of sin

The banging flywire door
I rattle keys in lashing rain
The meowing of the cat
Please sir give me more

I dump Whiskers ala Carte
Sardine le plain
I'm journey soaked
From fighting in the rain

The chair on which I sit
The trap that caught the rat
The saucepan which I heat
The cold and numbing feet
Outside the fright

Soup so warm
The purring from the floor
On another city night

Sardines for Breakfast

Inside the smells of sauce
My soul
Anyone's course peppered with salt
And funny things that itch

De-scaled de-railed headed tailed
I lay beside my fellow lost friends
Going through the bends
As ochre rust from in the corner of the tin
Reaching like the surreptitious nets that caught
The primary to the flaying of our flesh within

The darkness blacked me out miles ago
As I freely swam
Now stifled in this bed of tin
My spine where my chin had been
Valued life hardened with fat
Snack for some smacking lipped cat

Then a grinding sound brought the light
I flew away
My flesh a delectation in a moment
The smacking lips now cleaning paws
Now I soul the new spawns
In their absolute wonder
Such color such grace
As we all sing face to face

Wine and Cheese Women

Wine and cheese women on hot restless nights
Laughing and luring
Cavorting in caviar and obnoxious bubbles
Empty delights

Echoes in darkened door corridors
Facades behind
Intensities in motion blinding the blind

Redressed and polished in flush faced preparedness
Another man warmed for cost
Staccato violins and coarse rock and roll
Of cackling voices awaiting awareness
Prancing stilettos spiking souls lost

Smudged red on pastel cheeks
Crooked collars stains and wrinkles
Last minute groping with stub butted ashes
Numbness
Opaqueness
Problems with droops and keys that don't fit
Catching the catches the last minute silence
Devoured in cynical wit

Wine and cheese women staggering back
To sheets that crack and an empty door
Saddened yellow stares
Scattered red veins in eyes of blue
That gaze in a hollow at me and you

Supporting the wall swaying awash in gin
Upholding the past
All the men salacious grin
The real song - the one who could have made it
Enveloped her with love only to stray
Stamped on her heart
Sent her away

The wall fell down in a stutter
Her jellied legs crumpled
She began to weep
On a blackened thigh
Another ladder to climb
Wine and cheese women
Silently sigh
Sleep sleep sleep

What Happened in the Roman Baths?

They whispered in laughter tones
In an obscure corner of an opaque room
The smacking lips
The warm glows of nibbled necks in the quiet
Hot humming air
Nothing but steam in this Roman riot

Rampant sudden titters pierced somewhere
A ripping sound
Severed blood and a gurgling sigh
"The cow jumped over the moon"
People without a spoon without a care

Rolling misty vapor veiled whiffs of musk
The severed flaying arm in steam
High pitched masculine scream
And a very distraught woman whisked away
The elephant on the wall with tusk

Fifty years and one day later
A coarsely dressed man pushed an obscure door
In an obscure wall
He grunted in the spewing internal fog
Disappearing into the porthole view

An old lady scrubbed her last dishes
She collapsed dead in a deeply pitted armchair
Her coarsely dressed husband
Had stormed out smiling
With a satisfied nostril in full flare
Who knows why?

Goodbye Great Uncle and Aunt

Where you once preened now there is silence
Where you once dressed the shelves just wait
Where you both slept the dreams only echo
Dreams that once were laughter
Where once upon a time you were so

Frozen squirrels stand lonely now at the gateposts
Unmoved by all the little rubs you gave
Going out and in
Another generation laughs at the clowns
Admiring the crafted colored glass that smiles
Preaching your spirit within

The stories you told of jiving and war
Earls Court parties when Brylcream was slick
Spotted swirling skirts
Brash and bouncing
Sharp as a tack and more
Your red hair swirled on Liner Cruises
You were spiffing
On the Mediterranean dance floor

Pipe and smoke drew your breath away
Like your soul in the Synagogue of Freemasons
And that ring you used to flip upon your finger
Your joy and beauty and that laugh will stay
How could one forget at all?
Even your softness that showed
In benevolence and a pound or more
For a great great niece from a distant shore

I sleep over where you passed through the veil
Where we sort through all the stuff
I wonder if you peek back
Either by flame or light
At the inheritance you laid up
The portion heaven ordained for us
Throwing us into debtless freedom overnight

Little do you know
The windows that you have opened?
The souls that will bask in glory because of you
I wonder where you abide now
Since we prayed
For the beautiful view

The smell of history and a childhood long gone
Still linger
The Millennium beckons and your memory passes on
Into a death of another hundred years again
For just a little while in this world
Just another little song
My dears my dears for you I long

Package 5
FAMILY

'For this reason I bow my knees to the Father of
our Lord Jesus Christ, from whom the whole
family in heaven and earth is named'
Ephesians 3:14-15

BUNDLE 16

Home

The Lounge

Linear reds within geometric browns
Fluffy shag beige in soft deep eiderdown
Coppers I created with pots
Textured prints wooden frames
Bee's upon the ceiling mating
It's summer buzzing close to molded timbers
Soft to soothing sounds like simmering embers
Sitting feeling brown fit lithe and wealthy
Reflecting in the remembrance
Tippety taps…tippety tap…what is healthy?

Lampshade on body sculpted Oregon
African black
Candles flicker in their sunset hues
The Persian prince squinting affection
In rumbling sounds
Kamikaze Mosquitoes attacking the blues

Onyx rests on fellow stone with legs that cannot walk
Heads from faraway with classic British Dickens
Pickings of the past with dust
Like a puppet I turn my head
Bust of idol Buddha a soiled knife
Alligators skin all in a row
Green Mexican statuettes
The hall in silhouette
No other shadow

The limbs outside brush glass pluck holes in screens
Who cares flooding the moonlight in?
For flies and any other insect thing that swarm
Conical light gives credence to a cornice way above
Upon which rests this…security…this love
In a royal chair I sit a minority
In a fit of velvet red like satin sheets
So warm with tea

Fermenting in the Myriad

Orange hues of autumn stems and veins
Fragrant moods in a morning hush
Stillness in archaic time
Steaming crackling riverbed

Breakfast spirit rises
Birds with bells cockatoo's and friends
Whirling bending chatting

Two tooth tunnel master mulches grass
Honeyeaters pass to and fro with winks
A fetish in a masterpiece creating

Oh to breathe!
Oxygen by a lily world of golden streaks and mushy moss
The broken stone
Hue of blue in cracks
Where men have walked in ancient hours
Given to shoots and stalking stalks

Colonial tea garden lawns
Where canines yawned and sips were supped
Stables and vines wait patiently for steeds past
The ghostly neighing of mares and fillies
Capsules in the old wooden fence

Blooms of blinking browns
Blues in Bramante brusque
Magnificat!

Collage of petals in your hair
Snowflakes before the crisp and frost

Hearth on the winters night that came
Crackling face upon face
Picture upon picture
Thoughts and dreams
Remembered

Summer is a Gift

Summer a gift of serenity
Warmth that loves a silicon sandy beach
Drawing out stress
Casting it all to a living ocean
As we bask and brown out of reach

Summer a gift of simplicity
Accept the blooms before they fade away
Uncomplicated
Just enjoy the season of rest
Be the girl be the boy just have fun everyday

Summer a gift of now
Who needs knowledge of impending doom?
When the sky is blue and the sun is kind
When the rivers and oceans invite us with diamonds
Baptizing us anew to find

Summer is a gift to go
Home or by the sea to a pilgrimage of space
Away from all our creating
The human endeavor in the rat race
To stop and stand still
Breathe crystal breeze on sweeping downs
See further than ever from a lovely hill

Summer is a gift to spend
Ice creams whenever with kids as you explore
Something all encompassing you've never done before
Go out eat drink and be merry
It's an eternal joy from God
Summer is a gift
A gift from the Lord

The Welcomer

The House was welcoming
An absolute infinity of friends
But he who welcomed was welcoming with ice
Frost from unawareness
An unwelcome welcome

But He thought he was true and kind of truth
For the hearts of many who crossed that threshold
They came and went
As the Heights of the Wuthering

His inward mood was contrary
Overpowering the dancing
That continued without souls in sight

Strength and power in a mind apart
Searching past a level headed unchanging existence
For the limitless goal of the wonderful

The Welcomer's mind blocked the ties and barriers
Power which men felt and sheared away from
The challenge of faith at the ultimate crossroad

Who is the Welcomer?

Life cycles itself and things forget
People still smiled but were as close as grit
Ground hard into an inscribed doormat
Welcome?

The Welcoming heart and soul trekked about
Leaving questions holding answers

In the end though the immeasurable door will close
For a boundless goal cannot go on forever
Or can it?

There is a home eternal

Oasis

It has got to come
This level of God
Upcott to an Oasis
A place of pleasure
A home of fun
Love where the river runs

Seeking learning and playing
With doggies cats and donkey rides
A nursery and kiddy village
A place where one confides
Finding destiny and legacy the ownership of soil
The promised-land of milk
Brought with the price of faith
Brought unto the boil
Given with the grace
Sweet as honey and smooth as oil

Not just a home now
A field built where they will come to play and drink
Measuring your dream with theirs
Inspiring wisdom and more
Writing with pen and ink
A place to pray read and think
Study and see the future
Bring the melodies that will change the nations
Like wine mature
Before the time of expiration

Who wants a box when you can have a dream?
It's got to come this Oasis it's got to come
The children will return again and again
The memories will be warm
The bonds everlasting
Who wants just a house?
When you can have an oasis
Love where the river runs

Woman

Woman in a Ruby

Woman in a ruby
Looking through glass red
Willow in the window
Will it be said?

Will it open soon?
When my veil splits can I go and come?
To do my beckoning
Bringing evil undone

Woman in a ruby
Value far above
Shut in primary colors
Pierced in teeth and gum
Childlike in love
The red is on the run

Melody is flowing
Aloud my Spirit breathes
In my brown piano
Life and fallen leaves

Autumn glory yet to come
In spring when my dam bursts
When I rain and flood
The tide will shake everything
And you know the water hurts

Riding the last big one flooding all the shores
Wearing the ring that saves me
Breaking all the laws
Outside the red...
The woman in a ruby

Mothers

Dear Mothers
Clutch keys to the souls of sons and daughters
Sisters and brothers

In amniotic cup beneath matured hearts
She passes on within her rhythm
The universal wisdom of Him
Inherent cherchez la femme
The perpetuation of men

Umbilical severed
In a moment
But never of spirit

"Mummy, Mummy what shall I do?"
All is soothed all is quiet all is at peace
Tiny head blossoms receives a healing hand
Blooms lose their leaves in the shifting sand

Life builds its nest some strong and weak
Winds and storms come and go
Seen or unseen she protects
And moulds her yearning young
From valley to mountain peak

She always knows best who always knows
Whatever the word whatever the feeling
Whatever the distance she offers rest

Sons and daughters grow fruit
Some fall to the ground wrinkled and bruised
Others shine
Seen or unseen she draws them in
Creating in rhyme
Fresh growth and understanding
Healing guiding blessing
The fruit of her hands
Are praised between the gateposts
She's the gardener dressing

I am her son
Trained to run and not be faint
Never leaving I stand
I look to her eye to eye
A saint
Warm hand in mine secure
Strong and assured as the beautiful sky

Fashioned in her womb by hands invisible
She holds the keys of life and for her I sing
The wisdom spoken
Clothed in strength and honour
His perfect ring
Splendor that she is forever

Sons and daughters have grown
And mothers turn to dust
Her legacy living
Safely now we trust
She knew best
She always knew
Whatever the word whatever the feeling
Whatever the distance

Beautiful Glory

How beautiful my glory my strength
Shining in such shape that has formed you these years
Curves to bring Formula One to its knees
With burning rubber
Making ripe pears blush
Exclusive to me this rosy happiness by decree
In this checkered world to see you winning
The hands of a mother that the nations will honour
With beautiful glory

Battles have raged
And pain has rode your back to bow
But mountains have been high
Like the price at Christies
Nations have already heard of you
Heard the sound of coming glory
Seen the smile of purity
Touched by
The Shepherd la Femme
I know they will again.

It's never hard for you to feel the south wind
Explosion of oil in the garden of meandering pleasure
Knowing the trigger
Flick of tongue point of pressure
Brings you undone to deeply sleep
Without measure

On TV your beauty is even more beautiful
More like a Swede or Nordic princess
Fame licks its flame as the world calls and draws you
As water from wells the beautiful glory
Of a beautiful Lord in a difficult story
Your peeling bells will tell the truth
Ambassador of gorgeous possibilities

How beautiful my glory a book being written
Man smitten as years move on
So much time for the glue to dry
Planks from the eye remove
Seeing only the purpose of being enjoined
Fulfilling His dreams as sons of men
Killing the tares that woo

How beautiful again at twenty one
Thirty now nearly thirty one
You could be an angel
Despite the strife
My beautiful glory
Oh what a life!

BUNDLE 18
Children

Three Kah

Three
And in the silence of your concentration
Texta color soaks the printed outlined clown
Spilt paint way beyond the borders of his image
In your world of form from Spirit down
Dummy soothes
Your skin as cream
Full soft pink carbon of motherly lips
Frayed ruggy waits rumpled in its pretty pile
Crusty from runny noses dragged floors and slips
It's your comfort in a twinkle star dream

Three
And your little prayers are counted everyday
Little hands clasped
Little eyes clipped shut with a frown
"Jesus...that we preach the gospel and be in our hearts
Lord and devil go away...in Jesus name!"
In your little gown you know already it's not a game
Just like the prophet said
Kah is anointed to play this life
To slide with glee down His temple train

Three
We go for coffee
We like to talk dad n' daughter
McDonalds or a gingerbread man
Chocy shake ice-cream and flake
A treat everyday if you could
In every season
Why not it's for free!
You ask and you receive
From your obliging Daddy
But in the future vegan
You'll see

Three
You could be older
You nearly know all your numbers and the alphabet
Drawing letters
Things are taking shape
Little ones around you
Gather to the light of a leader
My little girl is running
Her eyes of blue are set
Three

Suck the Moon

The contorted teat wheezed spinning sounds
Like some sci-fi film
Crushed under infantile gums cutting molars
He drew deep like a puffer fish
Eyes to and fro in the cross beams of night
Milk like music swirled
As Jam sucked the moon

Son only son could be as beautiful as this
With golden hair so bright in my forearm cradle
Precious seed of so many smiles
And happiness yet to be
Peace in that warmth
Eyes as blue as sea

What you would die for...
What you cherish in your own reflection...
Father rising in the mystery of eternal programming
To and fro swaying "Silent night" singing
"Somewhere over the rainbow"
Telephone ringing as he sucked the moon

Mr Moo we call our son
One of those quirky names
We coin in our funny adult voice
"Moo moo man!" Poor kid...has no choice in this fun!
Little rosy cheeks balloon in that look
You know...the one you can't explain
That melts every mother's heart
Like singing in the rain
As you write this life of the little boy's book

Wrapped in a sheet like a straight jacket
Eyelids bounce toward sleep
The last of the moon eddies like a tide
Back and forth toward the plastic nipple teat
Concentration dissolves in that little world
No one has ever known about yet
He had sucked the moon and now was flying...

She Sings our Songs

She sings the songs on the way to school
Family melodies from heaven born
In the tough road of the prophet's call

She sings from deep within
These songs so crushed by evil light
I love this little girl of mine so far away tonight

The fight of faith has made me weary
What are these golden towers and TV preachers?
Sounding all the same as you surf
In this frequency of opportunities
In a clean and godly lonely Oklahoma place
Where tornadoes rip out hearts

I interview the famous ones with the millions at hand
But children still die
And sin eats the hordes with technological marvel
And people will always cry
I miss my little arrows
My precious Heaven's gifts
So way beyond all of this...

We seek direction miles apart her and I
For inside we die each day again
Purpose abounds but when

We seek a home
Hearts of fire that connect
Destiny we need
Mediocrity no more religion
Only one vision led by Him to heed
Our owner
Blood bought family
No not the Mafia
But sometimes you wonder!
When you see the trinkets of religion in Spain and...

The spirit ache is a deep pain
Thorn in the flesh on a buffet train
Won't go away won't leave you alone
Sucks your zeal through all its straws
Turning a soft heart into stone

The only answers left are much more of Him
A cliché over time
Ignore? A sin
There's no options when you know The Truth
No options when you know the truth
No options in
You must fly the eternal rim

So she sings our songs
We cry inside for her and him and her and more
Her wonderful little hands wring
In delight she looks up
Her little beautiful mouth pouts
Her tears taste so sweet
You just want the best don't you?

Jesikah and Watermelon

"Jesikah... you know...
God made Watermelon just for kids!"

I watch you running
Swimming without fear
Love in motion with a smile
Eyes so clear
Sounds of laughter defying the earth
Commanding a response
From the little ones
Ones who have not known the Light of Jesus
You then devour not one but 5 pieces
Uncomplicated slurps and giggles
Not a care in the world
Its buffet time in Spain and besides
God made watermelon for kids!

Jesikah you know...
If you draw an ES
Straighten the squiggle at the top
It's easy to make a 5
You are a winner and you know it
You live so alive
In moments you learn quick and forge ahead
Loving to draw
And at three your colors are so bold
Like red

Your numbers and letters dripping now
Your books of the future
Your art that will inspire
Your faith that will conquer
And Oh yes!
God made watermelon for kids!

He Who Loves Fun

My children don't walk they run
Eat life like food
Fight sleep till eyelids close the day
What a brood!

My children love the park so good
Simple things like sliding down
Swinging climbing trees
Touch wood!
Running laughing abundant in the sun
And a picnic even squeezed in between
Oh through a child's eyes must we come
To the beckoning Lord
He who loves fun

My children don't talk they shout
Even dream and imagine now
The house so small "Dad lets go out!"
Need an acre or two at least
Love them free to explore and paint prolific
Make sounds of many a drum
And melodies with a cheeky brow
Doesn't make sense but to some
Yet specific in how
Oh through my child's eyes I see a river and a feast
A waving hand beckoning to come dive and swim
It's He who loves fun

My children are a gift
Arrows being honed
Favor of God returned for my past dying
Born now in a womb of faith
As she is discovering her own in this sifting
Searching destiny of pain
Coming a long way at the end of the day
They lay eyes fixed to a box of characters
Interrupted by only dinner bath and bed

A tender prayer a cuddle
"Jesus loves me somewhere over the rainbow!"
Me oh my through my child's eyes
I love you
God bless sweet dreams goodnight son
I see open the oh so open arms
Gently they slip away to He who loves fun
So it seems so it really seems

The Fathers Love

We have got to have the Fathers love!
It is pure
It is whole
The grace is unending
The inevitable role

To find it you just have to walk
You just have to live the life
Who can teach you?
No one

You have to have the children
Experience it all yourself
The deepest of love
A realm that is veiled in the single world
Clubs rent and a shelf

Children are a heritage
They are a spiritual blessing and a gift
The ache of a Father and Mother
It's God himself – Love to live

We need it in the Church
No agendas no politics
But all the fruit of spirit
Such patience and kindness
Tenderness and thoughtfulness
Who can teach you?

Who can teach us of the Fathers love?
You just have to find it
Love and pain and the whole damn thing

Without it there is nothing but religion
Without it where are the children?
Without it the pews are empty
And the world parties on

The Lake

The Lake broods like the ducks at its side
Such peace so close to home
He leads me by the still waters
It's there my children roam and we have tea
Behind the hills yellow orange red
The sun begins to hide
Now it's dark the beauty is gone

We live in the hills and I work by the beach
The Rectory is paying the bills
But I reach and grapple with heaven
For my future beyond this comfort
The palm trees wave in the wind
Hosanna to the king upon a shallow shore

Jamin's treat day for doing all his chores
Kayaking and scooping the oars at five
We reach the little island of adventure and pirates
"Are there any crocodiles alive?"
"Of course there are!" I smile
He grabs his sister and I meet them on the other side
It was real for just a while

We all got wet and laughed and dreamed
The sun played the diamonds on this flat sea
Fish jumped to look as we skimmed
"Are there any sharks alive?"
"Of course there are" I smile
Behind the hills yellow orange red
The sun begins to hide
It was real for just a while

Now it's dark the beauty is gone
Why does it go so you have to fight and struggle?
The sounds of heaven laughter and peace
Are all you need
You sleep and escape another day

Tomorrow there are choices
And the scene is just the same
The lake is still flat and the fish still swim
It can all change in a moment in a whim

Princess

My Princess
Had I known I was a prince
As you waited in your tower
This priest and king was in the maze
When you were but a flower

I ran for heaven as you searched for gold
Looking for the white horse in flight
In its regal dress to sweep you up onto a mane of silk
While you were still crying out for milk
In a dark and wondering night

My dear soul and flesh
We all need that loving arm
The wings that keep us warm secure
When you braid your locks in sweet perfume
And dream of what could have been
Remember this imperfect prince loves alas
Always has in a silent room unseen

Princess I can see your tower
See you peering through a turret into a future
In the wind your long hair spins
I live down in the wild forest that surrounds that wall
I wait in patience for there is always a time
When the white horse rears to fulfill its call
But most of all princess
There is love, hope and faith that wins

Time ticks on princess
What has been has been
There are angels all around you
And a prince you have not seen
He is there waiting
One day princess one day
You'll ride the white horse
One day

Package 6
PILGRIMAGE

'Blessed is the man whose strength is in You, whose heart is set on pilgrimage. As they pass through the Valley of Baca, they make it a spring. The rain also covers it with pools. They go from strength to strength, every one of them appears before God in Zion' Psalm 84:5-7

Pressure

No Love and Pressure

My heart is still and I feel no pulse
Yet I breathe anyway
I see and blow bubbles with my gum
Chewing forty years of thoughts
In a cage my blood runs
Swiftly through grand central behind my ribs
Nothing of consequence rides the silent red

Doors have closed
With 'do not disturb' hanging string on a knob
Yet I'm disturbed seeking the favor
In a time of being robbed
Difficult times of adjusting culture for two please
Frustration on the side not much dressing
Penicillin in a dish with mold and furry bits

Truth in my palm
More salt for love's eluded feeling
Peace in the eye
But the storm doesn't lick the wounds or move them
The enemies of thought crush my rocks
In their eternal hard labor
It's time for parole and home for the calm

You do the expected
Never really know the fine line of sin
Grace everlasting never doubt that
Brass clouds making a terrible din
The heavens have elected
You keep on and pray anyway

No pulse in the red that used to surge as a flame
You know as you dream and remember
October November and the babe will come
A new life a new love a new one
Pulse in the new red
The name
Love and pressure it's all the same

It's there just buried under a pile of months
Of changes and carving roads
Doing the will
Tired but still
On top
Getting a life
Testing our hearts
In all the strife

Want to touch and feel and smile with ease
Drink in the garden again
Turn the fountain on again
Really feel again
Blow a bubble and pop

Stress

Sharp nails
Drive at angles into my head
Mexican waves of pins piercing
Dancing on my body
Leaving me for dead
Unseen needles relieving me of life through tiny holes
Faith fades in flying months
Where have all the flowers gone?

Will there be enough when all the things are right?
Will weariness rob what's left of joy?
The road never seems to end
For the man and the boy
If it's not one thing it's two or three
But never nothing
Never stillness and contentment for me
Because it never ends
The long time passing

Crackling on the roast pink skin on my eyes
Sore and dry
More wrinkles than a crow's foot
In sleep I never reach the basement of solitude
I wake but rest has passed
Eye cream
On a chimney full of soot
Oh please the eye cream!

On the Edge

Slipping
Grasping for rope
Signals bouncing in my mind
No sense and confusion
Fading light and dim hope

Every nerve tender
Every noise a wedge
Every thought an effort
Tottering on the edge

It comes and goes morning and night
Not fear but grief and failure
Could I be in a dream on a derailed train?
Carrying a theme with passengers of pain?

Every day I ache
I yearn for the love from Truth
Illusive yet I know
I just see the backs of men
Where is the purity of snow?

BUNDLE 20
War

Third wave on the Nek at Gallipoli

Hush hush
The pounding hearts dangle in the waiting heat
Sweating
Praying in the brow of death

The quivering stakes in white knuckles
Waited for the leverage
That would send the leopard and the pack
Squirming and writhing
In the heated lash of cocky lead

Tanned and rippling
Blue eyes in the taunting memories of that sunset
Billy in the bush and Kookaburra's smiling
Wafting in the wind
The warmth of fragile touch
Simple tear shed as machine guns shred

In wrath Hell's fire claimed friend and foe
In a common cause to live
From grave to pit
Pit to grave
"She'll be coming round the mountain
When she comes!"
Sung and said it was so

In broiling blood veins pushed forth in haunched skin
Achilles ready
Insanity where common sense had been
Flexed in steel for the bronzes of remembrance
Anzacs bounding one by one
Knowing the death
Standing tall in the boiling heat of the Turkish sun

Jezebel

Jezebel gunned for the prophet
Charismatic grin and batting blue eyes
Bleached hair a beach
A tarpaulin over a den of control
Jealousy envy
Insecurity the toll
Pruning any blossom
Threatening to bloom further beyond her wilting way

"You're not needed here!" the demon spirit said
How right
Yet woefully wrong
Religion sucks the juice of human endeavor
Wrapping it in cool systems that don't take long

Bellowed and barked
Sin in your face
No room for real love
Not even grace

Jezebels everywhere
Watch the fingers in your hair
Apostles come
Unlock the lair that massacres
Expose the scum that seeks to destroy God's Church

Holy Spirit's on the run now
She'll be thrown from the wall soon
Fed to the dogs soon
Jezebel with her ugly makeup
Jezebel with his posturing pomp
Then we can all rake up the bits
And put them in the blender
End the Devil's romp

We will sing and open the heavens with joy

Shadows of Despair

Like a digging finger in the shadow of despair
A fathomless ache revolves
Carousel in a not so fun fair
The music grinding
A planet in a spin for a universe of vision
That has already tasted purpose
Has already been sent to mend
Hors d'oeuvre at a government banquet
Chilli on the tongue at fast's end

Champagne tears moisten the future
Despair echoes its cry
Deep inside the well
Moss and lichen falls
Dissolving like manna in hidden water dark
Nothing is dry
As the sound polishes the ancient walls

Strong ramparts in the shadows
Stronger in time
Ready soon
Fermenting like wine

A digging finger for the shadows of despair
Eyes of children in the sunken sockets of abuse and lack
Mothers on the verge
Of insanity and hopelessness
Peeking over the crack

There's a digging finger
A sword of gold and silver dust
Hilt of quality and craftsmanship
One that knows no rust
Mother in nations
The voice of queens
A banquet of kings
To the shadows of despair

BUNDLE 21
Calling

I'm a Hurricane

Fortunes in my wealth
Thousands with my name
Little ones as sheep
Let's all play a game
Nations nations nations
Come throw all the dice
It will fall where we intend
Warrior warrior
Mice mice

See how they run
Oh sword of silver dust
I will conquer all
Neutralize the rust
Of all the damaged little lives
Can you feel the breeze?
Pol Pot's dead in Hell
No more beaten children
No more damaged trees

The wind is moving whirling
Now I'm a hurricane
I'm a hurricane
I'm a hurricane
That is why I came
Yes that is why I came

Tulsa Dreams

Tulsa dreams and acres of education
Towers of healing and angels
That spin tornadoes for fun
They know the sun hides behind
Having a purpose for open heavens
What dreams the sons of faith what dreams?

People pray have prayed
Fifty years of global love
Of faith
The morale
Birthing of sons and daughters
Thousand times more from Father Oral

Old but young
A sent one that better made the planet spin
In faith
Oh! That word
But true
Where is the wraith?
Only songs of praise in shopping centers for you

There is a level here that few find
From the surviving in the grind
It's in a word
The Word
A secret that's reviving
Dig deep
Tulsa dream
What else is there?

Truth

I want to tell it shout it free
Sing and bring the pictures I see
Aware of forces so intense resisting me

Perceiving angels
Arms are locked like policemen in a riot
Holding back the hordes
Of sulfur smokin' rampant sin
That wants to kill
Cave my only head right in

There's a possibility that this pain of frustration
Purposes us to dig for finer soil
Find purer seed and hotter oil
Because no matter the mountains we climb
There are always further needs to find

I hate not being respected
Hate being treated with suspicion
Like my agenda is against a vision
I hate the control of insecurities
Jealousy and politicking
I hate it with a passion
Jezebel's a massacre
Hell is pecking Hell is picking by the shed load
Like wars and a meagre ration

With me it's not an issue
I have a love of Christ so deep
Sometimes you know I weep
Certain facets have gone hard
Over forty now can't be bothered
With the fight at times it seems
To hell with this surviving
I love my kids I love the rhymes
The strength found in courageous times
I've got to get a life in reams

The dreams
Such a cliché in the race
But a desperate truth for a desperate cry
The greatest visions
They just all but die
Fading in the light of my child's pretty face

I just can't believe I feel this way
Man is a snare or so they say
But perhaps I must stay inside the mountain
Stay inside and sing
His Word makes me soar
Like a fountain washing clean

My mind is stirred
I think with knowledge that can change the world
I drink beer in a pub
Even Pharisee's hated that
I stand at the crossroads of Samaria
I think of a well having cappuccinos
How I would like to dive in
Resist the temptation to give up but swim
What radical ways are there ahead
For my babies and me?
Through these dark glasses I can see

Her towers of strongholds
She sees more than she sees
Nations hold out their arms
And say "Come Princess sing all your songs to us
Feed our babies with oil joy and gladness
With your foil of melody"

Truth and Ruth is pregnant now
God is pregnant now
He is hurt
His Church is a shadow of what it should be
How can I be this ambassador?
A man with a voice
A force with a choice
To affect nations and many a city?

It's a pity religion sucks our face
Shuts the doors on Martin Luthers
Sucks at our hearts
Sucks our blood
Sucks the Word
Sucks our race
Sucks in general really

I don't really know but I must trust
For my heart aches for truth but...
Everyone has agendas
Love and truth is a pure thing
We find it with a price tag
That would make the richest man shudder
And church bells ring

London encroaches and infests
In Australia cockroaches invade the kitchen
Day and night
You feel the itching
You want to scratch
Can we go on to glory in an imperfect world?
Are we in the slips to catch

We make programs we write scripts
We whip ourselves in our imperfect states
Flagellates
I want to climb the mountain
I want to achieve the ultimate
I really want to
I really want the truth ok
That's where the veil rips

No Voice

High above the highlight of my year
Before millennium
Where I sang for Him at the Royal Albert Hall
A door swings back and forth in the wind open
Hinges creaking
The cracked lock long gone
Another entrance here for the hosts
All because of the final mystery in our song

A surreptitious shape of a Pirates ship
Swirling masses of dark satanic cloud
Making threats to close what none can shut now
Unseen barriers of resonance repels
Sounds of a song in notes of gold so loud
Echoes of a wry ancient old wise wrinkled brow
Weapons undiscovered by religious shrouds
And stupid bells

Talons grip my throat later
No voice to tell as demonic pressure sucks my heart
Rough as an Alligators back
And ulcers that stab my taste
Tingles of needles as stress seeks to depart
Forty-one years now
And I'm dreading any more waste

She hates religion
Like having no money
This sweet wooing system lies to you
My favorite team won the treble
Man U
But the honey doesn't last
When the jar's empty you're through
Transferred on the market
You're just another product a memory past
Who are you?

I've had a big voice
But I'm wondering
You need to be fitter to hold up the sword here
It gets all so heavy and unnecessary

Things are starting to scramble now Lord hear
To many things to consider
Distractions and fracturing of time
The killing fields of momentum
It's all upside over dear
The ladder here goes down not up as you climb

I'm tired
No voice
It's not so bad
I don't have to do things out of duty or must
I can listen
Think and try to be at peace
From all the religious fads
I could rust away but my seed needs watering
I could stay unfulfilled but that would be so
Unfulfilling

I have always been willing and able
Like Abel not Cain
I want to feel the success
I need to stand in the warm rain
I was born to have a voice
To lead or at least do something significant
The Devil hops about with his ranting his raving
He's such a pain a sycophant
I have no choice but give
Considering the ant

My daughter brings home cress
She grew it herself at school
But I have no voice to say well done darling
No one says it to me but there is no rule
I have to become what I need to be

Fathers are few
And there's only One Who rings True

His ways are weird compared to the sweet system
The sweet cystem
The sweet cistern
Sisterin Satanin
Tea that stains my melee stress
It woos but hates the no voice
The system does
Killing choice

I'll be healed
Please voice fly again
Let's make it fine
We want it pure and unadulterated
Don't we my bairn?
Don't we
Don't we my wine?

Maybe just maybe it's red and over
Like His shouting blood revealed
It will come out of no voice I prophesy
This is my cry my cry my cry
Sealed
Selah
Catcher in the Rye

Less of Me

Dig the mud from my mossy wells
On these manicured lawns rake away the stones
Weed the weeds from all my beds
Stoke my coals that barely ember
When I should be burning
In heavens consuming hearth
In my eyeballs blue those flames reflect

Unsear my conscience burnt with iron cast
Blinded by the steam of seeing
In my weakness
Let Your strength
All your life to speak from me
Mine eyes be light and single
Undeterred by fear of men
That they may see less of me

Trawl my heart for hidden splinters
Scan my mind of worldly kosmos
Hanging me by the neck
Time after time
Fish on the hook line upon line

Thank-you for the thorns that pierce
That prick with needles crusty dust
Turning to Your face I can
Eye to eye cheek to cheek
Hand to hand to You we turn we must

Break the jawbones of my foes
Re-arrange my heart and soul
Smash my tongue with heated coal
Don't hold back Your perfect work
Prepare me for the kiln of truth
The Highlands sing the song of clans
I can hear Your song for me
Your tender hand extending nigh
That I may live The Truth and kill the lie

For You I long from this unpleasant tent
I long for ownership dominion all
Not to dance in tattered clothes for rent

I call my Lover Lord
King Warrior Friend and Brother
The cosmopolitan mix of sundry heavens
There is no other

Take all my leaven that falsifies this loaf of bread
My incense I yearn to fill the air
But pure must it surely be
Aroma sweet smell for You
So dig it deep my beautiful reverent King
And let it be less of me

The Prophets Journey - Zarephath

Spoke a word long ago
Words and more
Long hot days and desert sand
Nowhere is home to belong?
To have a life be keen and sure
There are no clues in the desert
Just heat sand and endless sky

Spoke a piercing word
One that shifted clouds and blue
Now I wonder about bread and water
Its source much more clear and true
The clues were in the son of the woman
Endless simplicities of baking and late moons

Spoke many words over years
Get a bit tired of them can spoil
His smile and her squeals
General chores around that house of oil

Being a dad being a prophet all the same
The clue's the rhyme and how you play the game

Spoke soothing words and she grew
She gave many pots of flour
So good to me warm and tender
Amazing the right challenge on the hour
I found clues in a simple touch
Washing up and warm stories at night

He came all of a sudden with a word
The battle was ready I had been primed
Me or no-one it was my job
The prophet's Big Ben coughed and chimed
She and her hordes waited blocking the ancient well
I waxed the sword to cut the Carmel heads
Send them all to hell

Cave

I Wondered

I wondered at death
I was snatching up that cross daily
In desperation deep in tears
Over attachments and emotions
At times I had clearly lost my breath
I walked and roamed the manicured green
Where my children played in spaces like oceans gone
Fears of losing dreams
As the Lark sings her song to me

I wondered at my deep pain
Peeled open like a yogurt pot
Feelings stirred in new ease now
As a gun trigger pressed
Just a look a smell a word in the rain
Love of extra fathoms coming
Father feeling husband loving
Alone so alone the smell of burning flesh
In separation there's something running
Forged so spry and at liberty
I know I love this nation
As the Wind sings His songs to me

I wondered over what is important
Family and fun
To be in love
Not undone in pressure in stress and burning candles
To pay the food and the rent
Entrenched here in eternal cold and TV
Markets conditioning minds
Beers and wines to numb a soul
No resources to reach the call and the goal
Before its time I know I love this nation
There is a song and a sound to be from me

I wondered about my son today
Jamin and his dad to cuddle
To sit with and to play
Bearing a security and love
Simply enjoying everyday
Jesikah and Chelsea
The girls who need my arms
Banner wings to teach and be
The highest of my call over all the urgent things
To romp laugh and huddle free
There is a new song to sing to see

I wondered
How deep can love be carved
In pain the adversity has no doubt much gain
But what a road!
What a loss!
He who loves His life...!

So much buried in her yesterdays
And the confusions of tomorrow
Battle scared by Jezebel
Who comes to crush and massacre
Depress and kill - defuse and discourage so

There is a timing there must be a timing when
The children love to play to play
The Lark sings again and again

Under the Ice

Under the ice the air is cold
There is only you
The sky is blue under the ice
Here we tread water trying to breathe
Waiting patiently and obediently
Waiting sometimes bereaved
My skin is at the mercy of shriveling before its time

We share air staying alive
Swimming in circles like strong sharks ready
Autumn comes and the leaves grow crisp
I like the rich crunch there was always a risk
And the fact you have to clean them up
To avoid drowning
It reminds me of gathering and prospering
Like the dream we dream under the ice

Under the ice the hole must come mustn't it?
Like the door into heaven
Like the door into the movie theatre
Where you watch the dream and write the revelation
Where billions read and misread knowing but never ever

I want our ticket now
Because my wetsuit needs the warmth of the sun
My bank account needs the warmth of the Son
My life needs the warmth of love and care
My children need the best of truth it's only fair
They need fun and space and laughter and freedom
Not the maintaining streams of steel under the frozen ice

This is a place for seals and fish
And other crazies who wish to dwell here
Stupid religious hats and frocks
With dangly cocks of seed with no support
Ho! Is that...?
I can hear the walking boots of salvation
On crusty snow
Reeling in His line to kill the show

I'm hooked and I can't get off
Don't want to really
Beyond weary
Enough is enough
Under the ice it must be over now
Break over apprenticeship ended? Thanks Sting
Let's get out of here before I die in the thaw
Now that's silly because you must and it's true
What? Die for the Lord of the ring?
Yes!
Then you're free to belong wholly to Him
Happens under the ice you know
It happens under the ice
So beautiful there is the color blue

The blues
New shoes
Big poo's

There is the price under the ice
Anyone can of course but few do
Like really...
The road out of the hole is narrow and few find it
We want it under the ice
Above the ice...
I mean way above
Like viewing the marble earth from the moon
When He ascended with captives and gave gifts
Creating new shifts in all the rifts

Now He promises amazing things
That most average Joe's don't know
We've asked we have faith we have given
We have been faithful as best we know how
We have been driven
Controlled used and abused
We have failed
We have become weak
We are not in debt
We are organized the best we know how

We...we...we can't do anything else but wait
As David said, "I say wait"
P27 a door to heaven
So ok Dave we do
It keeps coming in
That's money just
We're breathing through a straw though
We are close
We have to be
It's tough
It's the world inherited
Benefactor time
Come to the Oasis beat out a rhyme
Through the hole a bruised knee
Into the promise
Into the era
Out from under the ice
Like you know I mean out and never going back
Smash the mirror
That's the plea

Tree Song

I hear the wind blow a song in the trees
I sit with tears and memories
My pores ache with the stress of wanting
The sound of clapping leaves soothe
The song sings of peace
I am here
Green is love
I dare not move

Rejoice and leap for joy
They excluded your fathers too
It's hard not to cry at the memories
Of everything you do

Losing Faith

She shrinks and fades away
I watch and pray sometimes helpless
A prune sits on a kitchen bench
Her faith oscillates so hapless
What can I say to its injured roots?
Wounded deep unable to settle
To be at peace in this confronting world

Doesn't want to live doesn't want to die
Then another day wants to ride the sky
Then hell beneath spits its fumes
In a tossed soul the pendulum swings
She just has to ask - be humble
To be entire lacking nothing

The drive of an old upbringing pushes hard
Yet motivation for everything fades
Dead but alive
Seeing that it's good is a gift
Every seed must die to bear big
It's the way of the universe
She sees but does not see
Locked in an inward shell
Fragile as eggs treading water in an abyss

Jezebel pushed and drove the fear
A hand me down from the family tree
Of religion that said you could not dance
You could not when you should have been
It resisted the men
It challenged the faith
Which had already won
It stopped the momentum toward destiny
Killing innocent passion for the Son

There are many second chances
With grace mercy and favor
"According to your faith" the Master said
It does not take much just a seed
To shrink to fade to leave

To run give up to die is all an illusion
When we choose to believe the impossible
Which isn't that bad a solution

Bali blows another ground zero with New York
There are more rumors of war
Black Metal preaches its antichrist
We all dream of nice houses and white SUV's
Being comfortable in a Zion of gum trees
Sand and rolling surf by the shopping centers
Woe

The Devil's hiss makes you fade
Being washed in the wrong water on the wrong cycle
Makes a fine jumper lose its size
To then only fit a child
Shrinking fading losing dying letting go
Coming to the end
Being humbled broken exposed and bruised
To be healed to trust again
In Him alone
To change a screwed world
Is worth losing faith

To lose is gain as is dying
But better to be present walking the journey
Smelling the valley of Baca
Committed to the pilgrimage
Despite the state of the road

Money is paper houses created from soil and wood
Cars come from the ground and burn oil
He made anyway
A nation is a drop in His bucket
What is man that He thinks about us all of the time
Especially when we fade shrink and lose
What is precious
Our faith

He always has a new seed in His bag
The size of the moon on your pinkie
That's all it takes to do the works

Just believe said Jesus
Just believe
Losing will be winning
You will see

Where?

Where can I walk?
Where can I wander?
Where do I plant?
Where do I ponder?

I step on the glass
I drink from the vine
I press in the fast
Seeking a sign

What could have been?
Grieving the time
When the ships that I sailed
Slipped from my rhyme

The ache of the lost
The prosperity
Many at peace now
Except you and me

Where do we go to my lovely?
When we are alone in our bed
My roots need a home for the goodness
That constantly swims in my head
Where are the pools that are deep?
Where are the hearts that are fair?
Where do we go to my lovely?
The things that we need are so rare

Searching for Me

A room locked up?
Nay a house
Latches tight
Shutters jammed so
Blocking out the light

I run and hide
I ache and shout
Thrown away the keys long ago
I can't get in I can't get out
I'm a boat without a row

On the porch I swing
Back and forth going where?
Waiting for the post
The phone
The online invitation to bring me home
Taking all I have inside
To all who sit in pews and hide

That day the heart burst
Wounds and arrows
That robbed my fortune
And killed my sparrows
It came pouring out
But worse the pain
My spine collapses yet again

I'm alone in search of me
The paint peels
My house is locked
Yet the key I have is real

Package 7
PRESENCE

You will show me the path of life; In Your presence is fullness of joy; At your right hand are pleasures forevermore' Psalm 16:11

Present

The Finest

The moon shines full on all
The sun plays games on the flood
I am clothed in the finest of linen
I am washed in the finest of blood

With a crispness of air I breathe
With a torrent of tears I cry
We pray prayers to bare the deep
We look boldly on and die

I am not afraid to keep
I AM that rips the veil
I am a patriot of the King
We walk and then we wail

In pain I lit that moon
In pain I heat the sun
I cannot wash that blood away
It has already been done

The linen white billows free
The Egyptian wisdom dead in me
What purpose are their clothes but one
To take the journey to the Son

His Finest is in what we walk
The finest... if we only knew
It's over the years we realize
It's only the Finest of the Lord
Only the finest will do

Frames

Faith frames the world
Through the words of surprise
Pictures are clear confounding the lies
In a gallery of stars where the colors collect
Only The Book can wholly connect

A pastiche of strokes from all the Masters
Van Gogh's brush was too small for Mars
I can hear his ear hearing
Aching for heaven
In the beautiful room of Arles

The alphabet sows many lines
Of sand and sea lands and skies
Sets the boundaries of nations times
For purposes to actualize

Frames are for looking
Through windows doors and gates
Faith lets you see beyond
The loud voices of your mates

Frames mount the wall
Creates atmospheres
The call to you all
Is from your prophets and peers

Come off the hooks the auctions are ready
The things you will do
The things you make steady
You will change you will change
I guarantee
As you frame your world with the gift that is free

The Presence

"Dad won't you lay down?"
I'll be too old for this
Before you can frown

"Dad won't you lay down?"
Unwrapped the package now
For the next thirty years
Hundreds and thousands
Drowning in beers

"Dad won't you lay down?"
The essence of worship
The smile of a clown
The presence of God is coming to town

"Dad won't you lay down?"
Prayer and a cuddle
The world cries for love
In all of its muddle

"Dad won't you lay down?"
The love of my son
Sing and stroke hair
Sleep from the fun the fun sinking to more fun...Zzzz
Dreams of the fair the merry old fair...Zzzz

"Roll up roll up!
Hear the music of the carousel
Hum it together as you go round and round
Riding white horses laughing out loud
It's yummy candy floss in My dream
In a dream a dream can you feel My presence?
In the dream
Soon it will be living real dear son
Ace in the slipstream
Icing and fresh cream the world undone
Tell Daddy tell the daddies soon son"

Holding my boy I wake up at dawn
Rested and light the enemies gone
My final poem a bundle of joy
The presence of God is all over my boy

"Dad you should have seen…
It was beautiful Dad
It's what it's all about!"
We write from the river
And quell all the doubt

"Dad won't you lay down?"
This is where you're undone
It's the heart of love
The heart of worship
The love of the Son

This anthology finishes to begin again
"Dad won't you lay down?"
That's the package I need to send
Need to send

Yes Jamin – goodnight!

THE END

ABOUT THE AUTHOR

Stephen Bennett is a multi-creative; author, poet, singer, songwriter, worship leader, recording artist, and has produced Christian television, film, and documentary programs. Poetry has been an expression of his life journey since he was a teenager. He loves seeing artists rise up, fulfilling their art, blessed by God, and prospering in their craft. Stephen has traveled widely, encouraging and inspiring many singers, musicians, and artists. Nearly 40 years a Christian, he continues to write books, produce, teach, and be a creative voice. Stephen is from Sydney Australia.

CONTACTS

Write, message, or email:
PO Box 1312 Dee Why
Sydney NSW 2099 Australia
Email: stephenbennettbooks@gmail.com
YT, TV programs: awesomecitytv
Blog: youcanchangeyou.wordpress
Instagram: @youcanchangeyou
Facebook: Stephen Bennett

OTHER BOOKS

By Stephen Bennett
The Divine Artist - *Art for God's Sake*
The Poetry Packages - *Thirty Years*
Prepare and Arise - *It's Time for the Nations*
Prophet Musician 2.0